ALIGNING

By

PERSONOGEN

PART ONE

PART TWO

PART ONE

Why Align to Self?

What is aligning to self?

Hatred is conditional love, imposing, limiting, fierce, focused on impossible. Acceptance and ALIGNING is unconditional love, pivoted on POSSIBLE. These are the polarities of person. On one extreme, there is mental construct, blocking POSSIBLE, CONNECTION and peace. On the other extreme, there is balance: mind, heart, strength are ONE.

There are three kinds of aligning that each aligns with one of the three different persons, which comprise our entire PERSON. The three persons that comprise our PERSON are the BE (HEART/GEN), The Do(Strength/Generator), and the reflective(mind/witness). The BE is called GEN. The Do is called The Generator. The reflective is called the witness.

It is possible to align with our own point of view, our own mood, our own reflection, our own silences, or our own rhythm. This is called mirroring, contemplation, thinking. This is aligning with our witness, the reflective person of the three persons in our triad that makes a PERSON.

It is also possible to Align with our own Doer or Generator. When we align with the Doer, we are Aligning with our own Decisions, our own Roles, our own Performances of these Roles, our own Mover, our own Shaker, and our own Rainmaker. We Align like this when we do things we enjoy or imagine. When we make life happen, we are Aligning with our own Generator, our own Doer.

It is also POSSIBLE to ALIGN with our own CORE, or GEN. When we ALIGN with our own CORE, we access our own SOURCE of POSSIBLE. When we activate our own SOURCE of POSSIBLE, we overcome our fears, imprisoning constructs, sad reflections and more. Our CORE makes everything POSSIBLE. If we access POSSIBLE toward what we actually want, it becomes more possible. If we access POSSIBLE away from what we do not want, it also becomes more POSSIBLE.

Accessing our CORE activates balance. When this balance is activated, all three persons are mutually aware, appreciative and cooperative with one another in balance. They become ONE.

When a person comes in balance (aligned), they become truly confident and relaxed in all circumstances. When we imagine how to make things POSSIBLE for another or ourselves, we naturally align with them and within ourselves. Aligning requires a reach, deeply grounded in POSSIBLE.

ALIGNING WITH SELF- BALANCE

When we get out of balance, our three persons that comprise ONE, when in balance, deny the existence of one another, jockey for prime position and challenge validity of one another. When we are out of balance, we tend to forget decisions we have made as our own decisions. This is because our witness(reflective/observer) is ignoring our Generator (Decider). When we are on the move, making things happen with less reflection, we can often lose track of why we are doing what we are doing in the first place. Our Generator is ignoring our witness.

When witness and Generator acknowledge one another, we become more balanced. We allow our observations and thoughts to inform our actions. Yet ultimate balance is not found until they unite in POSSIBLE, GEN. Then the two access the GEN and we move from bi-polarity, to an OUR that is tri-polar. The witness and Generator become aware of GEN in POSSIBLE. Yet the first two still jockey to be most important. All have incomparable importance. All are most important. So until it is decided by Generator and considered and observed by witness that GEN is MOST HIGH of all of our persons the three remain tri-polar. When GEN is MOST HIGH, ORIGIN and SOURCE of the three, they become trigenic aware and instantly balance as three in ONE. TRUE ALIGNING is when we align in POSSIBLE, with the CORE of PERSON. This means all three of our persons are in balance to be one PERSON.

Inner conflict is resolved in balance. Stress is relieved. POSSIBLE dissolves stuck impossible(s) away. Hope is created.

Balance

Once we gain balance, we can approach others in balance. When we approach other while out of balance, it is imposing. Some of these impositions can take the form of forceful emanations, stalking, pressure, lectures, over-analysis, entitlement, neediness, desperation, loneliness, drooling, emotional absence, whining, complaining, secrecy, fear, absence, psychological distance, suffocation, rules, ultimatums, trades, enforced agreements, superiority contests, abuse, ignorance, or indifference.

When someone in balance approaches another person, it leads to aligning, POSSIBLE, sharing and unified vision.

Deciding something is impossible or unwanted is a kind of exclusion, which begins self exclusion once more. Comparing something as better or worse is an indication that balance has been challenged with a polarity.

Priority- MOST HIGH

Imbalance is the result of three persons remaining apparently divided and fractured in the estimation of two of those persons. Each person is important, incomparably so. Yet two of these three persons are vying for ultimate position over one another and the GEN. The GEN never seeks conflict or contests the value of the other two persons, which are integral to ITSELF. The GEN is always balanced. When the other two persons, the witness and Generator, access the GEN, they both become relaxed and balanced. While accessing the GEN, they appreciate and cooperate with one another. Their confusion stops. They come into balance and the three become ONE.

Which person is most important: GEN, Generator or witness? They are all incomparably important and essential persons with unique perspective in a PERSON. Which is MOST HIGH? Which should be the first reach of all persons, to find clear perspective and balance?

Only the reach towards the GEN (POSSIBLE) provides balance and ends contest.

Most Original

      The GEN is ORIGIN, SOURCE, MOST HIGH, MOST REAL PERSON of all persons that comprise our being. If reality is that which is neither derivative, nor dependent, finding the most real would be to seek that which is most original and most independent. If Generator comes from GEN, accessing POSSIBLE for everything Generated and witness comes from GEN, accessing POSSIBLE for everything reflected, then it follows that GEN is SOURCE for both. GEN is ORIGIN for all POSSIBLE that comprise witness and Generator. So GEN is the most REAL.

Most Independent

GEN exists independent of Generator and witness, yet Generator and witness are dependent on GEN for SOURCE of POSSIBLE. This makes GEN the most independent person of our three persons that, when in balance, comprise us as ONE PERSON.

GEN

GEN is the PURE, CORE, CONNECTED SOURCE of POSSIBLE that is ONE of our three persons. When GEN is accessed for POSSIBLE, all three are brought into balance, which can lead to ONENESS of self.

CONNECTED/UNITED AT CORE LEVEL TO EVERY PERSON

At our CORE, we are invisibly connected to all persons in existence. Our external and decided connections are created through our Generator, assessed and confirmed by our witness.

A BABY BORN IN POSSIBLE

    All babies are born fearless. Everything is POSSIBLE. Fear, Anger, Expectation, Prestige, comparable I and My are all learned impossible(s). The infant begins in the place of PURE POSSIBLE.

INNER CONFLICT: SOURCE OF POSSIBLE VS. DECIDED
IMPOSSIBLE

From infant in POSSIBLE we are taught the impossible. We learn our fears, taught for safety. We learn our optics, taught for manners and social awareness. We learn rejection and exclusion, taught from emanating tactics for protection from others. These are all learned impossible(s). Impossible(s) are attempts to aim away from a POSSIBLE in the future. Yet aim away from always polarizes what we do not truly want. This can have the effect of inner conflict, wanting and not wanting simultaneous. Once the target we want to miss is considered, we have accessed POSSIBLE to call it into being. Then when we decide we do not want it, we Generate an impossible, which conflicts with the POSSIBLE that has been accessed.

We also experience acceptance, embracing, accommodating needs, aligning and love. These are rooted in POSSIBLE. These we aim at directly. There is no polarization or feedback.

When an impossible is considered and a POSSIBLE is considered simultaneously that melts it as necessary, inner conflict and anxiety are dissolved. For example, a young boy is thinking about his growing football abilities and tells his two closest friends, "We are going to make it to the Superbowl someday." Another boy overhears the possibility and announces, "That is very unlikely and actually impossible." The boy looks down sad. His friends are sad as well. Then the boy looks up again, right into the bully's face and says, "Why not?" He smiles, "With my increased speed and increased completions, my times will rival professional times substantially by the time I reach college." His friends laugh, nod and agree. The bully disappears.

TURNED TO IMPOSSIBLE

Once we have turned away from POSSIBLE and find ourselves living in a rather stuck impossible, our story begins. How are we going to get out of this corner? Is this all there is to life? How can we be so stuck, yet stuck we remain until POSSIBLE is imagined or accessed once more.

TURNING BACK TO POSSIBLE

Once we are stuck in the Actual, it is possible to believe that Actual is more real than POSSIBLE. Yet everything Actual, actually came from POSSIBLE. First it had to be possible, then Actualized. When we look at what is Actual and have lost sight of Actual having always come from the POSSIBLE, then we feel stuck. We are cut off from accessing POSSIBLE once more for Actual to evolve flexibly. Once we turn from impossible and access POSSIBLE, Actual merges with POSSIBLE and impossible melts into POSSIBLE once more. Our future seems flexible, no longer stuck or stagnant.

STORY

Story is about how a person who is stuck, gets unstuck. Story is about how a person facing a challenge that seems impossible, finds POSSIBLE inside themselves to melt this challenge into achievement. The consistent Dominion over apparent impossible is called character.

Why Only a Person Can Have Story

Only a person has POSSIBLE as their CORE. Only a person can get stuck in an apparent impossible, disconnected from their CORE. Only a person can turn back to access their CORE and melt their previous problems away with POSSIBLE.

If a person never turned away from POSSIBLE, got stuck and lost, then there is no story. If a person only stays stuck or only gets more stuck, there is no story. If a person is stuck and turns toward POSSIBLE from an impossible fixed position, the listener, audience and story sharer, feels this POSSIBLE in themselves as emerging, when they watch it emerge in another person. Story creates aligning and sharing. For a moment, we are ONE with the character's journey from stuck to POSSIBLE.

PART TWO

ALIGNING WITH OTHERS

The reason we crave aligning within ourselves and with another person is to actualize the unity that already exists at our CORE level between our persons in ourselves and between another person and ourselves. Story is when we have turned away from unity towards impossible, fractured, fear, blocked, imprisoned, worried, anxious and lonely pieces of ourselves that once were ONE.

ALIGNING, TRUE ALIGNING is turning back towards POSSIBLE, the clarifying of connection, the relief of reunion and ONE. Perhaps it is better to state that balance is the natural state and disposition when a human PERSON is in alignment with all of its persons, namely Heart(Be), Mind(Do) and Witness(See).

How does one learn aligning? Can one person study another person to serve them or become more pleasing to them? Is it possible to become pleasing to the eyes, the ears, the taste, the scent, the touch, the imagination, the mind and more? Becoming pleasing is one kind of aligning. It is aligning to the senses, constructs and optics of another person. Is it possible to watch deeper and learn another's dreams, cravings, passions, rhythms, rituals, decisions, beliefs, pleasures, sensitivities and more?

Why would one person seek to align with another person? Why would one person refuse to align with another person?

How is aligning achieved? What are the steps? Is aligning difficult to learn? Are some persons more difficult to align to than others?

PERSONS in balance, always align naturally. Persons out of balance tend to feel loss of self, replaceable, less prestige, etc, when they "lower" themself to align with another person they feel is beneath them. Similarly, when a person who is out of balance seeks association with someone they feel is above them, they feel insecure, competitive, fear, out of place and embarrassed.

Aligning is the one true way we acknowledge, navigate and embrace others, their decisions, their beliefs, goals, dreams their desires and their everything and approach adopting these decisions, beliefs, goals, dreams and desires as our own. In Aligning, we acknowledge every person is same as us at their CORE. Their journeys to their CORE are diverse, yet all of our CORE and all of our destinations is essentially the same.

Aligning is the deepest kind of connection one human being can have with another. True Aligning ends all contests and miscommunication. Both see one another as persons and move towards more and more POSSIBLE together.

Agreeing

Some may mistake agreeing for aligning.

It is true that in all aligning, there is agreement. Yet it is surprisingly also true that in all agreement, there is not necessarily aligning. This happens because sometimes people construct a decided version of a person in their mind and agree with something that is not a person at all. It is a miss.

So it is perhaps best to align with the true person through possible and then agreement will flow naturally.

Obeying

Some mistake obedience for aligning.

It is true that in aligning, there is always obedience, flexibly so. Yet it is not necessarily true that in all obedience there is aligning. Just as in agreeing, it is possible to relate to an artificial version of a person we have constructed to represent them to us in our mind. This construct can inhibit us from being able to hear the person directly. It can lead to miscommunication and disobedience in the most fundamental ways.

Believing

Believing alone is perhaps a decision. That is perhaps a discussion for another time. Yet believing with someone is sometimes aligning. Similar to agreeing and obeying, all aligning has agreement in believing, yet not all agreement in believing has aligning. Sometimes people agree linguistically and have fundamentally different meanings in linguistics. Aligning solves for this because it remains flexible, reaching and open to adjustment. It is firmly rooted in POSSIBLE so it is easy to imagine that both apparently divergent beliefs could be one.

Try to think of one example of believing that has NO amount of deciding.

Knowing

Try to name one example of knowing with absolutely NO amount of believing. This isn't about not knowing. This is about finding where knowing comes from originally. Every example of knowing has believing at its source.

Now try to name one example of believing that has absolutely NO amount of deciding. This isn't about discarding believing, it is about understanding it more fully. Do we create our beliefs through decisions? What is real?

Reality is that which is neither derivative, nor dependent. Reality is the most original and independent level. So knowing is derived from believing. Believing is derived from deciding. This makes knowing a derivative of believing, which makes believing more real, more original, the source of knowing. Similarly, believing is real, yet it is derived from deciding. So deciding is more real, the source of believing.

What is the source of deciding? What is the SOURCE of POSSIBLE decisions?

The SOURCE of POSSIBLE, from which all derivatives flow, is your GEN, according to "Personogeny", a book that discusses the powers and composition of person.

Yet in the array of reality, ranging from derivative to most original essence of being, knowing and believing are definitely derivative. POSSIBLE is ORIGIN. So the most original, most independent person of ourselves is our SOURCE OF POSSIBLE. Knowing is real. We feel it, decide it. Yet, knowing is less real than the believing that created the knowledge to be remembered and moved forward in time.

Believing is real. We experience our beliefs very deeply and profoundly. We defend them even with our lives in some cases. Yet the decision is the Origin, from which Believing is derived.

The decision that "we believe" is real, yet this decision is less real than the decider who made the decision. The decider is a real role. Yet, the decider role is less real than the possibilities that the decider sources, from which he will ultimately decide.

Aligning with the knowledge of another person must align with our decision, our beliefs and our knowing. Yet since we have the capability to edit or discard decisions that no longer serve us, perhaps aligning is more possible than originally believed.

Affirming

Affirming is different than believing, knowing or deciding. Of course we do decide to affirm, yet affirming itself is a decision to agree with a belief. It is a response. Affirming is an aligning "gesture" to agree to something that has been stated, asked or implied by another.

Following

It takes aligning, referencing another for shifting trajectory of direction and intention, to follow another. Following creates belonging at some level to the idea, group or regimen one follows. Others who follow the same idea, group or regimen recognize you as belonging with them at some level.

Leading

It takes aligning, referencing a follower for shifting trajectory of direction and intention referencing and following your own trajectory, decision and intent, to lead. Learning to lead requires great capacity for inspiration and aligning.

Anticipating

True Anticipating is only possible after careful study of a person and their various trajectories of want, belief, craving, desire, dreams, aspirations, regimen, ritual, need, connections, standards, protocols, instructions and silent expectations. Anticipation can be surface and based on assumptions that miss the true trajectory of another and becomes an imposition. True Anticipation is always present in Aligning, where it sources possible trajectories and then narrows down on the more likely ever-shifting trajectory.

CONNECTED IN CONSTRUCT

We are all naturally connected at our CORE, SOURCE of POSSIBLE, immeasurably SAME, PURE in ESSENCE and more. We are connected in our Construct through shared Decisions, Beliefs, Knowledge, Brand and Identity. Our invisible world is connected in essence and construct. Our visible world is connected through construct alone. We have to decide if we are connected in the constructed, decided parts of ourselves. Our CORE connection, however, is inalienable.

Connection Observed

Some say that connection either happens or it doesn't. Yet do they allow it to happen if the person is unacceptable to them for any reason? No. So denying your decision in connection is simply about being unaware of yourself.

Connection Created By Decision

All connection is created by decision. Can you imagine ANY connection where you had absolutely NO part in accepting, embracing or sustaining that connection? It really isn't possible. Once you turn your focus to that connection and consider it, you decide if it is true and you want it to continue or if it is disconnected and you want to mend it or discard it. If you decide to continue a connection, you are affirming it once more and strengthening your decision that it should be kept and carried forward through time. This is a construct. Some call it a relationship.

Conflicts Between Creating Connection and Other Decisions

      Sometimes we create decisions that conflict with other decisions. When both decisions are attempting to co-exist, this causes stress and less satisfying completion of these decisions.

Connected OR Independent

   Some polarize connection and fight their ability to connect. If I connect, I cannot be truly independent, they reason. So they block themselves from connection to keep their freedom. Yet isn't it possible to be completely free and be connected? Aren't they still connected to their friends?

Connected AND Independent

Aligning isn't about challenging the self-sovereignty of another person. It isn't about surrendering your own self-sovereignty. Self-sovereignty is inalienable, at your core, and cannot be surrendered. It can appear to be surrendered in an adopted role, far from your core, as a pretense. True Aligning is about conceiving possible with another person in the face of apparent "impossible". Aligning creates story. It connects two persons in the possible to make a WE, an OUR, where before there only existed an I or a My.

Personifying Connection

Each person is comprised of three distinct persons that when harmonized through POSSIBLE become ONE WHOLE PERSON. When we connect to another person, we usually align with one person at a time. Sometimes we align with what they reflect upon, agree with their assessment. This is aligning with their witness. Sometimes we align with what they Do. We do it with them. This is their Generator. Sometimes we align with POSSIBLE with them. When we access their SOURCE of POSSIBLE, all of their persons align into ONE and ALL of our persons align into ONE. When we align with possible with another person, our self-sovereignty is joined with theirs in SHARED SOVEREIGNTY. This is ALIGNING.

Aligning with the witness

The witness person within us is reflective. It observes, considers and assesses with its own inner generator. This is a passive/active generator within the witness itself. This generator is distinct from the Generator of our whole PERSON, which is its own person. This generator is subject to the witness.

Aligning with the Generator

Toddlers align with the Generator during parallel play. They see someone doing something and decide they will do it next to them in their own way. They are glancing over and getting ideas on their play from the other. This is still aligning as they are referencing the other continuously. When one or the other chooses to stop the play, the other will often stop and go to the other activity with them. Toddlers use a lot of their reflective selves to learn. They copy language, behaviors and gestures. Aligning with the Doer of another is aligning.

Aligning with the GEN

When we consider a perceived impossible of someone, and look past it together towards POSSIBLE, we are aligning with their GEN. The GEN is the SOURCE of SAME, POSSIBLE, CONNECTION, PURE, and STORY of a person. When we align with how we are the same as another, we align with that person and unite our persons into PERSON to join with them as PERSON. When we align with how anything is POSSIBLE, the same happens. When we align with how we are CONNECTED in ESSENCE, the same happens, etc.

Aligning with the WHOLE PERSON

Once we align with the GEN of another, their CORE, in any measure, their persons align with their GEN as well. The three (GEN, Generator and witness) become ONE. Our persons do the same. Then our PERSON and their PERSON, align as ONE.

I

Aligning is unlikely in the "I" construct. It is too singular. It references only awareness and reflection. It has less access to possible and actual. This means that thinking about aligning is not the same as ALIGNING. Just like thinking about loving someone and talking about loving someone and describing how much you love someone can be vast galaxies away from truly loving someone.

My

Aligning is less likely from the focus of "My". It is still possible if "My" is a role agreed to in the "OUR", then it is play. When two persons agree to pretend that one owns the other for sake of expressing passion, this is always in the context of understanding this as a role that a person can step into by choice.

A person is innately self-sovereign. Any choice by a person to enter a role that implies compelled or compulsory aligning, it must be clear that at the core, a person is still innately self sovereign and by their choice they may exit this role at will. We always belong, essentially, innately, and ultimately, to ourselves.

Our

Aligning is most possible in the "OUR". If one person is using the word "OUR" to create a sense of entitlement, possess a person and their possessions rather than OUR as a perspective to and from POSSIBLE. This is not a TRUE OUR. This is a derivative Our that creates imbalance and entitlement.

Aligning Focus on Same

Aligning is always present when our focus is on how we are the SAME at OUR CORE as another person. SAME creates aligning elements and great likelihood for kindness.

Comparable Same – Aligning

Comparing one to another for similarity is an act of ALIGNING.

Integration

Tracing derivatives back to origin is an act of aligning. Stalking reality always creates integration of extensions back into SOURCE, or ORIGIN.

Comparable Different – Diversity

Comparing to source differences dis-aligns us with other persons. It is possible to see differences and integrate into whole. Yet this process of seeking differences to create a reason for exclusion can be very dis-aligning and dis-integrating.

Disintegration

When a snake bites us and presses its poison into us, the poison interferes with our body's ability to stay unified and connected. The poison is said to have a dis-integrating effect. Seeking differences for purposes of exclusion is such a dis-integrating activity.

Comparable Different Creates Contest

Comparable differences that create "exclusion", create destructive contests. Contest.

Comparable Difference Creates Exclusion

When we compare another to ourselves for the purpose of proving ourselves better, or proving them better, both dis-align us from that person. We exclude them when we decide we are better. SAME is alienated. We exclude ourselves when we decide they are better. SAME is alienated. Aligning requires SAME and POSSIBLE to be in focus for Aligning to be successful.

Aligning Focus on Possible

Focus on POSSIBLE is always aligning. In any way we feel blocked, lost, fearful, stuck or excluded, we are experiencing decided "impossible(s)". When we turn our focus to POSSIBLE that melts these apparent impossible(s) into possible, we are ALIGNING with that person.

Anticipating By Trajectory

When we see a tower near the cookie jar and we see the child building the tower, we can approximate that the child may want a cookie. Asking the child if they want a cookie, clarifies the guessed trajectory. When we see a child get good grades and care about activities that would look good on a college application, we can get an idea that the child may have a trajectory towards college. When a gentleman takes a girl to the jewelry store to look at engagement rings, she may think he is thinking about marriage. If she asks him to confirm, she may be more certain. Trajectory is an approximate probable target. It is possible the gentleman is engaging to someone else, or teasing her in some fashion.

When we see repeated trajectories connected to inclinations, words or mannerisms of a person, it becomes possible to anticipate them in some measure. If the girl gets her nails done every Tuesday at 8PM, it is possible to find her there, if you are looking for her on Tuesday at 8PM. It is also possible to meet her there with flowers if you want to surprise her on your anniversary.

Increased Flexibility

Every time we let go of rigid constructs in favor of POSSIBLE, we increase our flexibility. GEN is RECEPTIVE, POSSIBLE, FLEXIBLE. Generator is flexible when one with the GEN. Witness is reflective, assessing and rigid when it gets out of touch with reflecting GEN. When witness only reflects itself and Generator, it gets stuck. When it reflects GEN once more, it becomes flexible and free.

THE RECEPTIVE PERSON

GEN is RECEPTIVE. It is purely PASSIVE, SOURCE of POSSIBLE.

THE REFLECTIVE PERSON

The witness is reflective, assessing.

THE ACTIVE PERSON

The Active Person is the Generator. It actualizes POSSIBLE from the GEN with calibration reflected from the witness. When the witness is ignored and the Generator seeks only its own minute witness built into it, it can become lost and stuck, unaware that it created its own constructs, beliefs or knowledge. It feels as if it was always there, just there.

THE WHOLE PERSON

When all three persons come into balance, or PERSON, they are aligned with the GEN, completely aware of one another and appreciating and accessing all for highest and best abilities. When GEN is held as MOST HIGH, both Generator and witness look to GEN (POSSIBLE) to calibrate and inform their activities. This keeps them all in balance.